DESIGNED
FOR
JOY

A guide for moving from anxiety and defeat to a life of courage, joy, peace and breakthrough by renewing your mind and understanding your identity in Christ

Val Petty

DESIGNED FOR JOY:

Copyright © 2020 by Val Petty

All rights reserved. This note booking journal may be reproduced for personal use only. You may not share this file with others without express written permission from the author.

Published by The Essential Joyologist Franklin, TN 37064.

Table of Contents

Special Thanks To v

Introduction 1

Chapter 1: Clarity 4

Chapter 2: Trust 18

Chapter 3: Identity 40

Chapter 4: The Trade 68

Chapter 5: Supernatural Sight 85

Resources 105

Connect with Me 107

Endnotes 108

Special Thanks To:

My husband Barrett: Thank you for continually listening to me as I worked through this writing process. Your encouragement and support means the world to me. I chose you thirteen years ago and I still choose you. I love you forever.

My kiddos, Mary-Townes and Drew: You have my whole heart and you are both a constant reminder of God's kindness to me. I am so proud of you and thankful for you. I pray that you always remember that you are worthy, valuable, and loved just as you are, and that your Mamma loves you to the moon and back.

My parents, Patti and Andy: I don't even know where to start. I'm fairly certain that there's never been more supportive and loving parents than you two. I learned joy, celebration, and courage from you. I hope when my children grow up, they enjoy being with me as much as Mary-Walker and I enjoy being with you.

My sister, Mary-Walker. I truly can't imagine life without a sister. You are my best friend forever and I'm so thankful we get to do life together every single day. Thank you for always supporting me, being my favorite, and giving me the most adorable nieces ever.

My soul sister, Jennifer: I am so grateful for your friendship. We have spent the last three years shifting and growing together, and this book is just a piece of the treasures we've mined. I've learned so much from you and I'm so thankful for all the times you've challenged my thoughts and "held my arms up" when I was tired. Cheers to us finding our joy and spreading it.

Introduction

There are more than 7,700 promises in the Bible. We are promised that God will be with us wherever we go, and that He will give us the peace that surpasses understanding in all circumstances. God promises to give us peace, love, and a sound mind, and He says He will provide everything we need according to the riches in Christ Jesus, We are commanded not to fear and to be strong and courageous, yet most people are living stressed and anxious lives.

I began writing this study a few months before the COVID-19 pandemic hit. Our collective levels of fear, anxiety, and stress were crazy high before the quarantine, but as fear circulated, I observed these levels hit a fever pitch. There was so much uncertainty and anxiety surrounding jobs, financial security, health worries, grief over life changes, and isolation from family and friends. I knew people needed to be reminded of truth more so than ever.

So I started an online study and walked some amazing women through the mind-renewing tools you'll learn about as you move through this book. It was such a gift to be able to lead these women, and as we wrapped up the five weeks, I asked them what they had gained from the experience. A few of the responses were that they had moved from feeling lost to hopeful, sinking to swimming, tired to rejuvenated, and defeated to empowered. Words like *freedom*, *renewed*, *refreshed*, *empowered*, *strengthened*, and *joy-filled* were used to describe how they felt when we finished.

Now, my prayer for you is that you will find joy and freedom in this renewal process too, that you will be set free from the lies your heart believes, and that you will see clearly your identity as a child of the King. With all the struggles around us, it's easy to become overwhelmed if we don't know who we are and whose we are. We are meant to thrive, not just survive. Focusing on who you are in Christ and applying these mind-renewal tools will change your perspective and allow you to experience the true joy we were designed to walk in.

Introduction

How to Use This Study

This study is designed to be meditated on and discussed with friends over the course of five weeks. You can meet with friends and work through the exercises one chapter at a time, or you could work through each chapter alone and come together to discuss what you personally learned from the experience.

You can certainly work through the book on your own and at your own pace, but I have found that something symbiotic happens when you work through it with others who are dedicated to the same journey.

However you choose to approach the process, please know that I am praying for you and I'm excited for you to find the joy you were designed to experience.

For extra support, you can find me on Instagram and Facebook at The Essential Joyologist or you can check out my podcast, *Metamorphosis,* which helps you release emotional baggage and embrace truth.

Chapter 1
Clarity

Let's rewind a couple of years. I was rounding the corner toward forty years old, and I was really struggling. I knew the Bible, and I had been in church for my entire life (well, except my college years when I chose to sleep in on Sundays). I prayed about everything, and I had seen God work miracles in my life.

I knew the Fruit of the Spirit from Galatians 5:22-23. As a believer with the Holy Spirit inside of me, I trusted that the fruit I could be experiencing in my life was divine love in all its varied expressions: joy that overflows, peace that subdues, patience that endures, kindness in action, a life full of virtue, faith that prevails, gentleness of heart, and strength of spirit. And this fruit was meant to be limitless.

Although I knew that was supposed to be my reality, at that point in my life I felt far from peaceful. I had zero idea how to achieve the peace God said was available to me. The gap between what God promised and what my reality felt like was big.

The previous nine years had been hard. I had dealt with miscarriages and infertility, and my marriage was really hard at times. I continually felt a lack of financial security, which led me to never feel like we had enough money. I had been a hair stylist for seventeen years, and while I loved my clients and the salon where I worked, I had been ready to move on for a long time. I had built a good business selling essential oils, but my feelings of financial insecurity led me to believe that I would never be able to stop doing hair. Overall, I felt unsupported and alone and trapped. Of course, I still had joy in my life. I loved my family and friends, but all of the hard things had me bracing for the next blow, anxious for what would come next.

The way I handled life struggles at this point was to go into action mode. We are all different, and some people retreat when faced with a life challenge. But I'm a fixer. I worked and pushed harder. If my finances felt tight, I took on more hair clients and tried harder to build my essential oil business. If there was a health issue, I researched and researched and learned everything I could about alternative solutions. When our marriage got hard, we went to marriage counseling. Suffice it to say, I was striving so hard and trying everything I could think of to solve my problems, but nothing seemed to be working. I had no peace. My thoughts ran in my head like a hamster on a wheel and it was exhausting. I was begging God to rescue me from my circumstances so I could find joy, peace, and courage to really start living. In other words, I felt like I couldn't experience the fruits of the spirit until God fixed everything I deemed wrong in my life.

Even though I wholeheartedly believed what God's Word said, my emotions about my circumstances were overriding my beliefs. In my head I believed that God was taking care of me, would provide for me, and was working things out for my good. I could quote the scriptures that backed it up, but my emotions about my circumstances left me feeling powerless, unsupported, and unloved. My heart was not in agreement with what I knew in my head to be true.

Unfortunately, the distress and exhaustion from being out of alignment with God's truth usually drives us to manage our negative emotions in a not-so-healthy way. Have you ever had a stressed-out day and soothed your emotions with carbs and sweets, or is it just me who does that? How about a glass or two of wine or zoning out on social media? Sometimes it can look like bursts of anger or giving up on what you want because it's easier to be apathetic than deal with hope deferred.

Clarity

❓ Can you relate?

_____
_____
_____
_____
_____

❓ Are circumstances in your life robbing you of peace?

_____
_____
_____
_____
_____

❓ What do you run to when you are feeling emotionally stressed and want to block out the discomfort?

_____
_____
_____
_____
_____

Here's the deal. Many of us never learned how to process our emotions. As we grow up, we learn how to suppress them and stuff them down, and then soothe them with chocolate or wine or whatever method you wrote down above. We do this instead of processing the uncomfortable emotions.

The truth is: the situations I was dealing with did suck . . . and the stuff you are dealing with sucks too! No one wants to feel lack, experience relationship issues, or feel stuck in a job they don't love. When disappointment surged over my circumstances, it was easy to spiral into shame over the fact that I didn't have the peace I was "supposed to feel" as a believer in Christ. I would think, *Maybe if I would just read my Bible more or do another Bible study and try harder, I would be able to find peace.* But these thoughts just made me feel like I wasn't good enough. When I couldn't seem to find a breakthrough no matter what I tried, I would give into apathy and decide that God must have been just "allowing" these circumstances in my life to teach me something.

One day, in a very apathetic state, I told God that I was finished searching for answers. If adulting was just trial after trial with no real breakthrough, I needed to know so I could mentally prepare myself for that reality. I also told Him that I didn't think that was really how He worked, so if He would open my eyes to a better way of doing things, I was open to learning. I knew that the tools I had been using to manage my life weren't working, so I needed a whole new way of operating. I was asking, seeking, and knocking. Matthew 7:7-8, says, "Ask, and the gift is yours. Seek, and you'll discover. Knock, and the door will be opened for you. For every persistent one will get what he asks for. Every persistent seeker will discover what he longs for. And everyone who knocks persistently will one day find an open door" (TPT).

From that day forward, God began to reveal to me a totally different way of processing and finding solutions with Him. Instead of pushing and striving and trying, I learned how to co-labor with Him and work through my issues. This book was birthed out of the tools I learned for untangling the lies I believed while also renewing my mind to truth.

It's time to let go of the thoughts and behaviors that don't align with God's truth. It's time to let God reframe your thoughts to His truth: you are a unique individual created by Him with purpose and power. Your awareness will be expanded on the goodness of God, your identity in Christ, and the limitless power He has given you because you have Christ living inside of you.

A vitally important piece of this puzzle is learning how to renew our minds. Romans 12:2 says to "be inwardly transformed by the Holy Spirit through a total reformation of how you think" (TPT), and 2 Corinthians 10:5 says, "We demolish arguments and every pretension that sets itself up against the knowledge of God, and we take captive every thought to make it obedient to Christ" (NIV). We may have these verses memorized, but unless we know how to practically apply them to our lives, we won't experience renewal and transformation. True transformation occurs when we learn how to take our thoughts captive and measure our emotions against what God says about us and our circumstances.

The book *Switch on Your Brain* by Dr. Caroline Leaf is a fascinating look at how our thoughts affect us physically and emotionally. She uses current scientific and medical research in the field of neuroscience to explain how we can change the programming and chemistry of our brain by gaining control of our thoughts and feelings. She says:

> Research shows that 75 to 98 percent of mental, physical, and behavioral illness comes from one's thought life. This staggering and eye-opening statistic means only 2 to 25 percent of mental and physical illnesses come from the environment and genes.[i]

Most of the time we function on auto-pilot, waiting for a circumstance to meet our expectations before we relax. For instance, if we think we have a potential bad health diagnosis, we can spin out of control with anxiety and wonder why God is letting the situation happen, choosing to stay in constant worry. The minute the doctor calls and gives a good report, we instantly regain our peace and claim that God is good. This is an exhausting cycle, and it's not what we were designed to experience as God's children. It's only when we allow Him to reshape our thoughts that we can access joy in the midst of *every* circumstance. And that's just what we are going to learn to do! So, let's get started . . .

Find Your Word Picture

When you are not used to analyzing your emotional state, it can be hard to find the words to explain what you are feeling. However, your brain knows exactly how you feel and it can paint a really nice picture to describe it. When I was really struggling, one morning, I was in that dreamy in-and-out state that happens when you are just waking up, and a picture popped in my head of a rat being held upside down by the tail. The rat was flipping and flailing and struggling, but it couldn't get away. It snapped me awake, and I knew that the picture I had just seen in my head was a word picture that described the way I felt about my life. I felt unsupported and vulnerable, and no matter how much I struggled I couldn't get freedom.

Interestingly, I was also having a lot of low back pain at that time. Foundational issues like financial stress and feeling unsupported will often show up as lower back pain. My body was taking the information from where I was holding my stress, and my mind turned that into being held like a rat. Often, we can identify the root of our negative emotions by recognizing where in our body they are manifesting.

As I have led people through the process of finding their word picture, I'm frequently amazed at what they discover about themselves. One of the precious women who did the study is a very powerful person. She has a demanding job, tends to juggle a million balls in the air at once, and she was feeling very overwhelmed by the demands on her. When she did the word picture exercise, she saw a picture of a one-man band. The burden of carrying the weight of the responsibilities she manages made her feel overwhelmed and incapable of getting rest.

Another woman who did this study is one of the sweetest souls I know. She is a mama to two young kids, a school counselor, and a great friend. In her word picture, she was in a room by herself with white walls. This helped her understand that she was lonely and felt lost to her purpose. This is such a common feeling among young mamas, and it's only when we become aware of the way our hearts feel that we can begin to process the emotions that are hiding under the surface.

So, let's find your word picture. Take three deep breaths. Think of the areas that stress you and make you feel anxious. Now use your imagination and think of a word picture to describe how you feel in your current circumstances.

This isn't about getting the right answer. Just close your eyes and go with the first thing you see. When you get your word picture open your eyes.

Clarity

❓ Describe the picture you saw?

_____
_____
_____
_____
_____
_____
_____
_____

❓ What does it mean to you?

_____
_____
_____
_____
_____
_____
_____
_____

Ok, now that you have your word picture, do you see that what you are feeling might not be aligned with God's truth? Maybe there is something you believe about your life that God could teach you differently. We have to realize the gap between how we feel and what God says is true.

My word picture clearly defined how I felt in my life. When I saw the rat, I started thinking about the scriptures that didn't line up with that description of me, and I made a list of the passages that refuted my feelings.

A few of the verses that spoke to my specific situation were:

- "God is our refuge and strength, an ever-present help in trouble." (Psalm 46:1-3)

- "The name of the Lord is a strong tower; the righteous run into it and are safe." (Proverbs 18:10)

- "Do not grieve, for the joy of the Lord is your strength." (Nehemiah 8:10)

- "And my God will supply every need of yours according to his riches in glory in Christ Jesus." (Philippians 4:19)

- "Have I not commanded you? Be strong and courageous. Do not be frightened, and do not be dismayed, for the Lord your God is with you wherever you go." (Joshua 1:9)

- "Fear not, for I am with you; be not dismayed, for I am your God; I will strengthen you, I will help you, I will uphold you with my righteous right hand." (Isaiah 41:10)

I knew that God had good plans for me because His Word said so. Jeremiah 29:11 says, "'For I know the plans I have for you,' declares the LORD, 'plans to prosper you and not to harm you, plans to give you hope and a future. Then you will call upon me and come and pray to me, and I will listen to you. You will seek me and find me when you seek me with all your heart'" (NIV).

Nowhere in Scripture does God say he wants us to be unhappy and frustrated. In fact, John 16:33 says:

. . . and everything I've taught you is so that the peace which is in me will be in you and will give you great confidence as you rest in me. For in this unbelieving world you will experience trouble and sorrows, but you must be courageous, for I have conquered the world!

This doesn't mean we should hang tight and it will be good when we get to heaven. We have access to His victory *now*, but we have to train our hearts and minds to see it. We live in a sin-filled world, so we will have trouble. But God says in Romans 8:28 that he will work *all things* together for our good. I've heard Pastor Kris Vallotton say that this means that in any and every circumstance of your life, if it's not good it's not the end.

God doesn't instantly reveal the good to us, but the good comes when we choose to believe His Word over what we currently see. Faith is the currency of heaven. Hebrews 11:1 says, "Faith shows the reality of what we hope for; it is the evidence of things we cannot see." We have to choose to believe His Word over what we see because faith is an action and that action unlocks breakthrough.

Healing Work

Now that you have your word picture and you realize the feelings you are dealing with, make a list of Bible verses that promise the opposite. If you are dealing with loneliness, make a list of God's promises to always be with you and never leave you. If you are struggling with grief, make a list of verses that promise you that God will turn your ashes into beauty and your mourning into joy. If you don't know where to start, Google them.

Come back to this page daily and marinate on God's good Word. Put a copy up on your bathroom mirror or refrigerator. Make this list your screen saver. Write it on your doorsteps. Whatever it takes to remind yourself that God has more for you.

Then, ask God to reveal more to you about your word picture and where those feelings are coming from. Is this something you have struggled with all your life or is it a new emotion? Do you have pain in your body that might indicate where you are holding your stress?

Break out your journal (or get one if you don't already have one) and record how you feel every single day! I was not a fan of journaling before I began working through this process. I thought as long as I didn't write things down, I couldn't be held responsible for them later, but the journaling process is invaluable. There's something about writing that is cathartic, and it will help you process as you pull the info out of your head and release it onto the page. Plus, you'll be able to look back a year from now and be in shock at how much you've grown and changed. I promise! Write out how you feel each day, what you are grateful for, and what it feels like when you focus on your Scripture list. Record the nuggets of truth God begins to reveal to you.

CHAPTER 2
Trust

At some point in your life, you have been taught something or believed something that doesn't line up with truth of who God is. A. W. Tozer says, "What comes into our minds when we think about God is the most important thing about us." ii

I want you to think about God for a minute. Don't worry about getting this right. We are just playing and using our imagination to gain awareness of our thoughts.

Trust

(?) Imagine that God is in a room and you are walking in to see Him. Where is He? Is He far or near? Are you able to come near Him? What's His expression? Is He stern or loving? Is He glad to see you?

_____
_____
_____
_____
_____
_____
_____
_____
_____

Two Baylor University professors wrote a book called *America's Four Gods* based on data from a comprehensive survey to break down how Americans view God. The book is based on the concept that what we believe about the role God plays in our daily lives has a tremendous effect on our worldviews.

The study revealed that only 22 percent of Americans believe that God is benevolent, or good, kind, and loving. These people define their relationship with Him as "a personal relationship, like a friendship, like a companionship." The other 78 percent found God to either be distant, authoritative, or critical. This means that these people found Him to be distant and disengaged, a power tyrant, , or always noticing the things we do wrong.iii

So, we can assume that 78 percent of Americans view their relationship with God as anxiety producing.

I find it heartbreaking that only 22 percent of Americans believe that God is good, kind, loving, and personal. Yet somewhere in the weeds of life, I had decided that I was unsupported, unloved, and alone. I knew God was good and loving, but as my negative experiences piled up I was struggling to view life through that lens.

So how does that end up happening to someone who has a strong background in faith and the Bible? How do we miss God's goodness? There are many reasons for this.

Lies

The enemy may try to steal, kill, and destroy but he is *not* creative. He is still using the same tactics he used since the beginning of creation. He has been working to get us to question who God is and what His motives are since the beginning of time.

Let's look at Genesis 3:1-6 so we can see clearly how he causes us to get off track:

Now the serpent was more crafty than any of the wild animals the LORD God had made. He said to the woman, *"Did God really say*, 'You must not eat from any tree in the garden'?"

The woman said to the serpent, "We may eat fruit from the trees in the garden, but God did say, 'You must not eat fruit from the tree that is in the middle of the garden, and you must not touch it, or you will die.'"

"You will not surely die," the serpent said to the woman. *"For God knows that when you eat of it your eyes will be opened, and you will be like God, knowing good and evil."*

When the woman saw that the fruit of the tree was good for food and pleasing to the eye, and also desirable for gaining wisdom, she took some and ate it. She also gave some to her husband, who was with her, and he ate it. (emphasis mine, NIV)

Satan loves to make us question God by suggesting that He's holding out on us ("did God really say"), whispering lies to us ("you will not suffer the consequences God said you would") or tempting us ("you deserve what you desire, even if it's not good for you").

It's the same with us. The lies suggested to us by the enemy are darts of poison that keep us from walking in our purpose and living a joyful life. The enemy's main goal is to break the relationship between us and God. He wants us to think that we don't have access to God and that we need something outside of ourselves to bring us joy, so we end up living our lives trying to find the satisfaction and purpose that is already our birthright as His children. Here are some of the most common lies that God's people hear from the enemy. It's critical that we recognize them in our lives, so that we can turn from hearing the lie to hearing the truth.

Life Influences

For those of us who have grown up learning about God from a young age, we tend to absorb what we are taught, whether the information is correct or not. For instance, if someone presented God to you as a rule keeper and a cruel punisher, you would be frightened of Him. Our parents, friends, pastors, and Sunday school teachers have a tremendous influence on the lens we view God through, and if their lens was foggy, there's a good chance your lens is foggy too.

Father Issues

If your relationship with your earthly father is or was challenging, that can greatly affect the way you see and relate to God the Father. For instance, if you felt that your earthly father didn't provide stability for you, it can be hard to see your Heavenly Father in that light. Or if your earthly father wasn't present, it can be hard to see your Heavenly Father as a constant presence in your life.

Trauma or Negative Life Experiences

When something traumatic happens to you or you have painful life experiences that you don't know how to reconcile, it is very easy to blame God and put up walls in your heart even if you don't realize that's what you are doing. The wounding allows us to question where He was and why He let it happen. It's not wrong to ask those questions. You can ask Him anything! But when we stay stuck there and don't work through the pain to find His goodness, it negatively affects us.

Trust

In order to move from your word picture to the place where you rest in the promises of God, you have to know that He is good and that He is for you. Why would you ever trust God with the details of your life if you think He's just going to zap you or criticize you? It's only when you know that God is 100 percent for you that you will trust Him to restore the broken places in your life.

Trusting God involves more than just knowing the scriptures that say He is good. It's about a deep, fulfilling, and beautiful relationship with Him in which you go beyond knowing about Him to tasting and seeing that He is good. Creating awareness in the areas where your filter is off concerning His goodness is vital as you work through this mind-renewal process.

As I began to unravel the thoughts I had about God that weren't in alignment with who He says He is, I was so excited to see that God is even better than I thought He was. I already thought He was good, but as I began understanding more about His nature I was able to give Him more of my heart.

In the next section we are going to look at the nature of God and a few of the names of God found in the Bible. Trying to define God out of thin air can feel overwhelming, but His nature is revealed all throughout Scripture in the meanings of His names. This will help us to solidify a correct understanding of who He is. This is crucial because your identity comes from Him, and in order to embrace who He says you are, you need to trust Him fully.

Psalm 103 says, "The LORD is compassionate and gracious, slow to anger, abounding in love . . . he does not treat us as our sins deserve or repay us according to our iniquities . . . as far as the east is from the west, so far has he removed our transgressions from us" (vs. 8-12, NIV).

The Ultimate Father

God is the ultimate Father who loves and cares for you. He has always and will always pursue you. The overarching narrative of the entire Bible is God creating order, humans falling into disorder, and God redeeming and restoring order. He is always coming after us to bring us back into relationship with Him. You can trust Him because His love for you is limitless.

God loves us with *agape* love. *Agape* love is not romantic love or friendship love. *Agape* love is only concerned with the greatest good of another. *Agape* isn't emotional or about feelings of attraction. Instead, it comes from the will as a choice. *Agape* love involves commitment and sacrifice and expects nothing in return.

Agape love, in the Bible, comes from God. God loves from an outpouring of who He is. As 1 John 4:8 states, "God is love [*agapos*]," meaning He is the source of *agape* love. His love is a complete sacrifice; it is an undeserved gift of His grace.[iv]

The highest demonstration of *agape* love was seen when God sent Jesus to die for us while we were still sinners. Our relationship with God is secure and attached because He is *agape* love.

Most of you are familiar with 1 Corinthians 13. You've heard it read at weddings, laying out a list of things that define *agape* love:

> Love is patient, love is kind. It does not envy, it does not boast, it is not proud. It does not dishonor others, it is not self-seeking, it is not easily angered, it keeps no record of wrongs. Love does not delight in evil but rejoices with the truth. It always protects, always trusts, always hopes, always perseveres. (vs 4-6, NIV)

This is God: He is patient and kind. He doesn't envy or boast and He's not proud. He doesn't dishonor others, isn't self-seeking, and isn't easily angered. He keeps no record of wrongs. He does not delight in evil, but He rejoices with the truth. He always protects, always trusts, always hopes, and always perseveres.

He sees us as His beloved because He sees Jesus in us. He is where we find peace, freedom, joy, love, acceptance, security, and alignment.

The Ultimate Creator

God spoke the world into existence with His words. He has creative solutions for every problem you have, but you have to be looking for them. He rarely does things the way we expect Him to. We often miss what He's doing because we've never been trained to think from His perspective. He sees the full picture that we only see partially. He knows the beginning from the end, and He is outside of time so His solutions can often be unusual and outside of the box.

He sees all of your personal issues and He has a plan to bring breakthrough, but it may look very different than you expect. It's only in trusting in His goodness that we can rest in His solutions. Being stuck, sad, and defeated does not bring Him glory. But leaning into Him, fighting battles His way, and walking into victory does bring Him glory. As a bonus, you get to experience the ultimate joy of knowing that the Creator of the universe wants to co-labor with you.

He Reveals Himself to Us

God is constantly revealing himself to His children. I used to think that, unless I heard God audibly, I wasn't hearing from Him at all. I've come to realize that sometimes His voice is audible, but God isn't limited by the English language. He might speak to you through dreams, visions, pictures, a movie, a book, the Bible, a friend, a teacher . . .

Occasionally, I'll think about a question I have for God, and the answer will come in a way that I never would have expected. A friend may call and tell me they've been thinking about me exactly when I need a boost of encouragement. I may be reading a passage of scripture and a verse will come alive that I've never noticed before. I've learned to notice and be grateful for these moments. The more you tune your antenna toward Him, the more you'll notice His direction and encouragement.

The Names of God in Psalm 23

God is limitless and cannot be contained by a name, but we are given clues to His nature through the various names given to Him in Scripture. In ancient Middle Eastern culture, a name had deep meaning because it revealed the nature or essence of the person. In this exercise, we are going to look at Psalm 23 (KJV).[v] Each verse of this well-loved passage points to a name of God. We are going to look at what each name means and then think about where God has shown us this aspect of His nature in our life.

Jehovah-Raah: The Lord is my Shepherd

"The Lord is my shepherd."

In verse 1 of Psalm 23, we see the name Jehovah-Raah. A shepherd's primary responsibility is the care and welfare of his flock. The sheep may wander, but the shepherd will do everything in his power to protect the sheep. A shepherd knows each of his sheep personally and will leave ninety-nine behind to go after one that is lost. That is who our God is.

When has God cared for you and guided you as a companion and friend?

_____
_____
_____

Do you see that God desires to know you personally and care for you intimately?

_____
_____
_____

Jehovah-Jireh: The Lord is my Provider

"I shall not want."

Jehovah-Jireh is the name given to God by Abraham in Genesis 22:14. God provided the ram for Abraham and Isaac right when they needed it. Likewise, you can trust Him to provide for you. The more we rely on God to provide for us, the more we will see His provision. God is working behind the scenes and He is arranging the details so they will work out exactly when we need them to.

When has God provided for you in the past?

_____

_____

_____

What do you need provision for right now? Share your thoughts with God.

_____

_____

_____

Jehovah-Shalom: The Lord is My Peace

"He maketh me to lie down in green pastures: he leadeth me beside the still waters."

The God of Peace will bring you comfort and strength when you are distressed. In Judges 6, we see God's goodness to Gideon as He reassured Gideon and gave him confirmation when he needed it. Gideon built an alter to the LORD in Judges 6:24 as a tribute to the God who brought him peace. God will bring calm to your chaos. He will speak to you and give you confirmation so you don't have to live in tension and anxiety.

When has God surrounded you and given you confirmation that He is with you?

_____

_____

_____

What chaos or distress are you experiencing right now that you need to ask God to bring peace to?

_____

_____

_____

Jehovah-Rophe: The Lord is My Healer

"He restoreth my soul."

In Exodus 15:26, God reveals Himself as the LORD who heals. He tells the Israelites to listen carefully to His words and to obey His commands in order to stay well. He restores us by healing us physically, mentally, and spiritually. In fact, God is healing you as you work through this study! Renewing your mind to His truth is always a healing balm.

When has God healed you spiritually, mentally, or physically in the past?

_____

_____

_____

Is there anything you currently need Him to heal or restore? Share your needs with Him.

_____

_____

_____

Jehovah-Tsidkenu: The Lord of Righteousness

"He leadeth me in paths of righteousness for His name's sake."

In the Old Testament, Jehovah Tsidkenu occurs twice. It is first used in Jeremiah 23:6 and points to the fact that the LORD is our Righteous Savior. God stands for us and provides us with His righteousness and justice because we have nothing to offer on our own. He is the one who provides victory and prosperity for us. God sees us as holy and valuable because He sees Jesus's righteousness in us and we fight our battles from a place of victory because of Jesus's victory.

How has God's righteousness covered you?

_____

_____

Do you see yourself as holy and valuable because you are covered in Jesus's righteousness?

_____

_____

Do you see that Jesus's victory allows you to live from a place of peace and victory?

_____

_____

Trust

Jehovah-Shammah: The Lord is There

"Yea, though I walk through the valley of the shadow of death I will fear no evil; for thou are with me."

Jehovah-Shammah is the name of God that was revealed in Ezekiel 48:35. He revealed this name at a time when Israel was in rebellion and in captivity. God was letting the Israelites know that He was with them and He would be in their future. In the same way, God is in your present and He is already in your future. We often live in fear of some looming future event and wonder how we will manage if and when "it" happens. Rest easy knowing that Jehovah-Shammah is already there and He will walk with you because He loves you.

God is already in your future. Does that comfort you?

_____

_____

_____

What worries do you have about the future that God could speak truth into?

_____

_____

_____

Jehovah-Ezer: The Lord, My Help

"Thy rod and thy staff they comfort me."

In Psalm 33:20, God is addressed as the LORD is our help. Jehovah-Ezer is often used to describe how God is our helper and our shield in our battles. God goes before us and covers our back when we are at war. As you follow His commands, you are safe and protected. You can trust Him and rely on Him.

What has God rescued you from in the past?

_____

_____

Does it bring you comfort to know that God will protect you?

_____

_____

Has He commanded you to move forward on something that you have been scared to do? If so, talk to Him about it. He is your Jehovah-Ezer and He will help you.

_____

_____

Jehovah Nissi: The Lord is My Banner

"Thou preparest a table before me in the presence of mine enemies."

The name Jehovah-Nissi was given to God after the Israelites defeated the Amalekites in battle in Exodus 17:15. The battle was strange. As long as Moses help up his hands, the Israelites were winning, but whenever he lowered his hands, the Israelites would start losing. When Moses got so tired that he couldn't hold his arms up anymore, Aaron and Hur held his arms up so Israel could win the battle. The bizarre way they won the battle made it obvious that God gave them the victory. In the same way, God has a strategy for you to get your breakthrough. He has the answers you need for victory.

What victories have you won in the past with God on your side?

_____

_____

What do you need victory in right now that God could give you a fresh strategy for?

_____

_____

Jehovah-M'Kaddesh: The Lord who Sanctifies

"Thou anointest my head with oil."

God reveals Himself as Jehovah M'Kaddesh in Leviticus 20:8. We are not holy on our own. He intervenes and sanctifies His children so that we can have salvation. We are given salvation freely, and from there, we walk the daily process of surrendering to His will so that we can be set aside for His purposes. This daily refining of our hearts trains us to be more like Him.

How are you choosing to let God refine you into alignment with Him?

_____

_____

_____

Are you asking God to order your steps each day?

_____

_____

_____

Jehovah-Manah: The Lord My Portion

"My cup runneth over."

Jehovah-Manah is the name given to God by David in Psalm 16:5. David says that the LORD is his portion and cup. The Hebrew word for portion can be translated as inheritance. Our inheritance is the Kingdom of God and the blessings that come with it. God gives us the desires of our hearts, more than we can ask or imagine. Our inheritance is bountiful and we can access His treasures now and we will continue to throughout eternity.

Have you ever prayed for something that you now have?

_____

_____

_____

Is there something you desire to see happen that you could ask God about?

_____

_____

_____

Jehovah-Cheleq: The Lord My Inheritance

"Surely goodness and mercy shall follow me all the days of my life: and I will dwell in the house of the Lord forever.

Lamentations 3:24 is where we see the LORD being referred to as Jehovah-Cheleq. This is another scripture speaking to the fact that God is our portion, or our inheritance. I love this so much because, once again, it's a reminder that we don't have to wait till we get to heaven to see His goodness and mercy. We get to see it *now,* all the days of our life. Look for it and you will find it.

Where do you see God's goodness and mercy in your life currently?

_____

_____

_____

Where have you seen it in the past?

_____

_____

_____

I hope this exercise on the names of God has helped you see Him through a clear lens. He is your shepherd, provider, shield, peace, healer, help, victory, and your inheritance. He is there for you and He loves you. Are you allowing God to show up in those ways for you?

If you don't like where you are in your relationship with God, this gap only shows you how much you have to gain. It's time to experience the goodness of God. We get to renew our minds so that we can believe and receive His goodness.

Healing Work

Spend time asking God to reveal more of Himself to you. Ask Him the hard questions that you have for Him. He can handle it, and He longs to show Himself to you so you can have the relationship you need to grow and thrive—the relationship you were designed to have.

Chapter 3
Identity

We've become aware of the gap between how we feel and what God promises us. We've looked at how important it is to taste and see God's goodness in order to will trust Him in all circumstances. Next we are going to look at our own identity in Christ.

We were created in the image of God, and our identity is that we are His children. The benefits of our inheritance—having a seat at His table—should factor into how we handle every aspect of our lives. With our identity in Christ, it's entirely possible to live a life of courage and joy, but in order to get there we need to see the gap between who God says we are and how we feel about ourselves so we can close that gap.

When I was struggling with my identity issues a couple years ago, I kept thinking, *Why can't I find solutions and create breakthroughs in the areas that make me feel out of control and frustrated? Why can't I get past these same circular issues? If God is good and I know He cares for me, will provide for me, is present with me, is my helper, and has a solution for every problem, then why am I not seeing change?*

Could it possibly have something to do with me? Might my thoughts be the issue? While this seems like it could have been discouraging to realize, it's actually incredibly empowering to take responsibility for the way we feel. Then we aren't waiting for something outside of ourselves to resolve before we begin to take the actions to change our lives.

In your lifetime you have accumulated emotional baggage. Whether it's lies of the enemy whispering shame and unworthiness to us or expectations put on us by others and ourselves (all the things we should do), we make choices about who we are and what we are capable of. We create little boxes that we comfortably fit ourselves into. We absorb the opinions of others, which is why we feel trapped when we try to create change in those areas. I've dealt with this personally and I've seen it over and over again in my essential oil business as I've worked with countless women to clear out their emotional baggage.

I've witnessed the pain that women carry from words said to them in childhood about their looks, weight, worth, and so on. When we grow up feeling like we don't measure up, the ramifications are huge. This realization led me to co-create a podcast with Jennifer Hawkins called *Metamorphosis*. Lies we hear in childhood are often the root of why we fight the same battles over and over again: anxiety, low self-worth, anger, broken relationships, addiction, and so on. The heavy and hopeless feelings that occur when we experience emotions like shame, victimization, abandonment, guilt, bitterness, and unworthiness limit our ability to change if we aren't aware that they are the main players in the emotional turmoil we feel.

We may know the verses about being forgiven, loved, and secure in Jesus, but if we feel weak, overwhelmed, beaten down, small, unworthy, or incapable, we are not going to operate out of our true identity as children of God. The way you see yourself matters because you will always live according to who you *feel* you are.

One of my favorite Bible friends is Gideon. He is the perfect example of what I'm talking about. In Judges 6, you get to see his encounter with God, and it's really awesome:

> The Israelites did evil in the eyes of the LORD, and for seven years he gave them into the hands of the Midianites. Because the power of Midian was so oppressive, the Israelites prepared shelters for themselves in mountain clefts, caves and strongholds. Whenever the Israelites planted their crops, the Midianites, Amalekites and other eastern peoples invaded the country. They camped on the land and ruined the crops all the way to Gaza and did not

Identity

spare a living thing for Israel, neither sheep nor cattle nor donkeys. They came up with their livestock and their tents like swarms of locusts. It was impossible to count them or their camels; they invaded the land to ravage it. Midian so impoverished the Israelites that they cried out to the LORD for help.

When the Israelites cried out to the LORD because of Midian, he sent them a prophet, who said, "This is what the LORD , the God of Israel, says: I brought you up out of Egypt, out of the land of slavery. I rescued you from the hand of the Egyptians. And I delivered you from the hand of all your oppressors; I drove them out before you and gave you their land. I said to you, 'I am the LORD your God; do not worship the gods of the Amorites, in whose land you live.' But you have not listened to me."

The angel of the LORD came and sat down under the oak in Ophrah that belonged to Joash the Abiezrite, where his son Gideon was threshing wheat in a winepress to keep it from the Midianites. When the angel of the LORD appeared to Gideon, he said, "The LORD is with you, mighty warrior."

"Pardon me, my lord," Gideon replied, "but if the LORD is with us, why has all this happened to us? Where are all his wonders that our ancestors told us about when they said, 'Did not the LORD bring us up out of Egypt?'

But now the LORD has abandoned us and given us into the hand of Midian."

The LORD turned to him and said, "Go in the strength you have and save Israel out of Midian's hand. Am I not sending you?"

"Pardon me, my lord," Gideon replied, "but how can I save Israel? My clan is the weakest in Manasseh, and I am the least in my family."

The LORD answered, "I will be with you, and you will strike down all the Midianites, leaving none alive."

Gideon replied, "If now I have found favor in your eyes, give me a sign that it is really you talking to me. Please do not go away until I come back and bring my offering and set it before you."

And the LORD said, "I will wait until you return."

Gideon went inside, prepared a young goat, and from an ephah of flour he made bread without yeast. Putting the meat in a basket and its broth in a pot, he brought them out and offered them to him under the oak.

The angel of God said to him, "Take the meat and the unleavened bread, place them on this rock, and pour out the broth." And Gideon did so. Then the angel of the Lord touched the meat and the unleavened bread with the tip of the staff that was in his hand. Fire flared from the rock, consuming the meat and the bread. And the angel of the

Identity

Lord disappeared. When Gideon realized that it was the angel of the Lord, he exclaimed, "Alas, Sovereign LORD ! I have seen the angel of the LORD face to face!"

But the LORD said to him, "Peace! Do not be afraid. You are not going to die."

So Gideon built an altar to the LORD there and called it The LORD Is Peace. To this day it stands in Ophrah of the Abiezrites.

That same night the LORD said to him, "Take the second bull from your father's herd, the one seven years old. Tear down your father's altar to Baal and cut down the Asherah pole beside it. Then build a proper kind of altar to the LORD your God on the top of this height. Using the wood of the Asherah pole that you cut down, offer the second bull as a burnt offering."

So Gideon took ten of his servants and did as the LORD told him. But because he was afraid of his family and the townspeople, he did it at night rather than in the daytime.

In the morning when the people of the town got up, there was Baal's altar, demolished, with the Asherah pole beside it cut down and the second bull sacrificed on the newly built altar!

They asked each other, "Who did this?"

When they carefully investigated, they were told, "Gideon son of Joash did it."

The people of the town demanded of Joash, "Bring out your son. He must die, because he has broken down Baal's altar and cut down the Asherah pole beside it."

But Joash replied to the hostile crowd around him, "Are you going to plead Baal's cause? Are you trying to save him? Whoever fights for him shall be put to death by morning! If Baal really is a god, he can defend himself when someone breaks down his altar." So because Gideon broke down Baal's altar, they gave him the name Jerub-Baal that day, saying, "Let Baal contend with him."

Now all the Midianites, Amalekites and other eastern peoples joined forces and crossed over the Jordan and camped in the Valley of Jezreel. Then the Spirit of the LORD came on Gideon, and he blew a trumpet, summoning the Abiezrites to follow him. He sent messengers throughout Manasseh, calling them to arms, and also into Asher, Zebulun and Naphtali, so that they too went up to meet them.

Gideon said to God, "If you will save Israel by my hand as you have promised— look, I will place a wool fleece on the threshing floor. If there is dew only on the fleece and all the ground is dry, then I will know that you will save Israel by my hand, as you said." And that is what happened. Gideon rose early the next day; he squeezed the fleece and wrung out the dew—a bowlful of water.

Identity

Gideon said to God, "Do not be angry with me. Let me make just one more request. Allow me one more test with the fleece, but this time make the fleece dry and let the ground be covered with dew." That night God did so. Only the fleece was dry; all the ground was covered with dew. (Judges 6, NIV)

What emotions do you think that Gideon is feeling?

_____
_____
_____
_____
_____

Have you ever asked, If the Lord is with me, why has all this happened to me?

_____
_____
_____
_____
_____

At this point in time, the Israelites had been tormented by the Midianites for seven long years. Everything has been stolen from them and they lived in constant fear. Do you think Gideon was experiencing feelings of abandonment, fear, anger, and unworthiness? He was hiding out in the wine press when God came to meet him. I love that Gideon is honest with God and he flat out asks Him where He has been. God reveals that what they were suffering was a consequence of their own choices.

Just like the Israelites, we also have a tendency to forget that there are consequences to poor choices. God will certainly bring restoration, but we may have to sit in our mess for a little while before He does.

God heard the prayers of the Israelites and is going to provide a solution. He tells Gideon that he is a mighty warrior and that he will be the answer to their prayers for relief. Gideon did not feel like a warrior, though. His circumstances had left him feeling victimized, frightened, abandoned, and insecure. Plus, he considered himself the "least" in his family. But God knew what Gideon was made of, and He called out the warrior in him. He tells Gideon that He will be with him, gives him confirmation three times, and promises him that he will succeed in taking down the Midianites.

God revealed to Gideon that his identity was the opposite of everything he believed about himself. Gideon could have chosen not to believe what God said about him and ignored His call on his life. The challenge Gideon faced was to act on something he didn't see or feel. That requires tremendous courage and faith in God.

Before we move on, I want to touch on the fact that God was willing to give Gideon confirmation three times when he asked for it. He could have just said, "Do it or else," but God loves us and He knows our hearts. He is willing to show us what we need to see in order to walk out our purpose . . . if we ask.

Your Identity in Christ

Just like Gideon, you also are a mighty warrior. You have a unique purpose that God is calling you to. Let's look into the warrior you are in Christ and what it means to have a seat at His table.

First Peter 2:9 says, "But you are a chosen people, a royal priesthood, a holy nation, God's special possession, that you may declare the praises of him who called you out of darkness into his wonderful light" (NIV). As a believer in Christ, this is who you are. Let's break this verse down so we can apply it practically.

You are Chosen

Before the beginning of time, God chose you. You were seen, pursued, and loved first. You did nothing to earn your position, but when you accepted Jesus, your identity and your reality changed immediately. You literally became a new creation. Second Corinthians 5:17 says, "Now, if anyone is enfolded into Christ, he has become an entirely new creation. All that is related to the old order has vanished. Behold, everything is fresh and new" (TPT).

You *were* a sinner but when you were saved by grace your nature changed entirely. Jesus lifted you from the authority of the enemy to His authority. Your nature changed from a sinner to one who is righteous because of Jesus. Now, is it possible for you to still sin? Yep . . . but it's no longer your nature. You are not a slave to your bad habits or painful patterns. Now you have the Holy Spirit inside of you, which means you have the power to change your story. You are not stuck. You have choices and you can live in freedom.

Do you feel capable of breaking old habits, or do you decide to change and then find yourself eventually back in your old, dead end patterns?

_____

_____

_____

If you're like me, you make the New Year's resolutions but three weeks later, the dreams for a better life get squished because breaking habits and changing patterns feels hard. Getting up at 5 AM to exercise seems like a great idea, but when the initial motivation wears off, it's easy to slip into old pattens of sleeping in and missing the work out even though you really desire to achieve that goal.

You are Royalty

You are the son or daughter of a King. You have been adopted into a royal position. Romans 8:16-17 says, "The Spirit Himself bears witness with our spirit that we are children of God, and if children, then heirs—heirs of God and joint heirs with Christ, if indeed we suffer with *Him,* that we may also be glorified together" (NKJV).

You are also the bride of Christ. You have also married into your royal position. You have access to the kingdom and the resources of the King. As a member of God's royal family, you have been given all of the rights and responsibilities that come with the position. Jesus's victory is also your victory. Luke 10:19 says, "I have given you authority to trample on snakes and scorpions and to overcome all the power of the enemy; nothing will harm you" (NIV). The Bible tells us that all we have to do is stand firm in God's truth and resist the enemy. He has no choice but to flee because you are a royal child of God.

Children who are born into a royal family know they are set apart. They are trained from birth to know they have value, authority, and purpose. They know they are protected and are called to serve and lead.

❓ Did you grow up learning that you have a special purpose from God?

_____

_____

_____

❓ Do you see yourself as royalty?

_____

_____

_____

❓ When you walk in a room, do you see that you are a solution carrier because you have Christ living inside of you? Or do you begin to feel insecure and see all the problems that could come up or find all the reasons why you aren't capable of wielding your authority?

_____

_____

_____

You are a Royal Priest

1 Peter 2:9 says that you are a royal priest, which means that you are fully capable of walking out the purpose He has for you. As a priest of the most high God, you are currently seated in heavenly places. Ephesians 2:6 says, "And God raised us up with Christ and seated us with him in the heavenly realms in Christ Jesus." This means you are a citizen of the kingdom of heaven and and also a citizen of the country you live in right now.

You are capable of doing hard things. And by hard things, I mean believing that you can do what God calls you to do. I think sometimes we put God in a box and think that if we ask Him what He wants us to do with our lives, He's going to call us to do something we don't want to do. What good father wants their kid to live a miserable life? That's not how God works. He will call you to a purpose that you will *love*. Whatever God has for you might not be easy, but it will be something that satisfies you and brings you joy. Somewhere tucked away in your heart, you have desires that were planted by Him, and He wants you to discover them and walk toward them. It wasn't easy for Gideon to do what he did, but I bet he much preferred knowing he was a mighty warrior than thinking he was the "least in his family."

❓ Are you willing to open your heart to His purpose? If so, ask Him what it is.

_____

_____

_____

❓ Do you feel unworthy of greatness? If so, why do you think that is?

_____

_____

_____

You are God's Special Possession

You are extremely valuable because you are made in the image of God and you are His. You are so valuable that Jesus gave His life for you. That is what you are worth. You are priceless. God believes in you and He wants to co-labor with you to bring the kingdom of heaven to earth. Ephesians 2:10 says, "For we are God's handiwork, created in Christ Jesus to do good works, which God prepared in advance for us to do."

Identity

We are so valuable that God has tasks for each of us so that things can be "on earth as they are in heaven." God has given us each different talents and abilities. The God who creates every single snowflake and fingerprint with their own unique design has most definitely created every one of His children with special abilities and gifts. We each have a unique calling and it is going to look different than someone else's. There is no need for comparison because every one of us has our own God-given gold inside of us.

I think this is especially hard in the social media world we live in, but it's been a factor in our lives since we were kids. We are constantly being measured and compared to our siblings, classmates, and co-workers. It's so natural to look at other people's progress and get discouraged because we don't have clarity.

What I found for myself is that when I began to own my identity in Christ and clean out my emotional baggage (which we will look at in more detail in the next chapter), I became clear on what God had gifted me with and the task He was calling me to in this season.

Do you compare yourself to others on social media?

_____

_____

_____

❓ Do you wonder why they can do things you can't, or why they are progressing and you aren't?

___

❓ Do you feel shame and unworthiness over this?

___

❓ Does the discouragement cause you to doubt your gifts or shut down?

___

❓ How do you deal with those emotions?

___

Identity

You Are Forgiven

You received complete forgiveness in Christ and it is total and finished. Jesus paid it all because He loves you and He is Love. Romans 8:1-2 says, "Therefore, there is now *no* condemnation for those who are in Christ Jesus, because through Christ Jesus the law of the Spirit who gives life has set you free from the law of sin and death" (NIV, emphasis mine).

When you rehearse your sin, it is *you doing it*. Feeling guilt over past sins that you've already asked forgiveness for is a choice you are making. God is not the one reminding you. If you continually think over your previous sins, you are viewing yourself through the wrong lens.

Do you know and accept that you are completely forgiven?

_____
_____
_____

Do the choices of your past continue to haunt you? If so,

_____
_____
_____

You are a Warrior

In Genesis 1:28 God told Adam and Eve to subdue the earth, and Ephesians 6:10-18 tells us to put on the full armor of God. Why would we need to subdue and wear armor if we aren't in a battle? We have an enemy who longs to bring destruction and chaos to the order and beauty of the original design of God's creation and purpose. Ephesians 6:12 says, "For our struggle is not against flesh and blood, but against the rulers, against the authorities, against the powers of this dark world and against the spiritual forces of evil in the heavenly realms" (NIV).

Spiritual warfare is real, but you do not have to be a helpless victim to it. You are not a victim! You are not powerless! You have authority! You are prepared for every battle because you are a warrior in God's army.

It is the delight of the enemy to make sure your identity in Christ stays concealed so you don't uncover your purpose and stay defeated. Satan loves it when you are trapped under lies and emotional turmoil because those things keep you stuck.

So what do we do about it? We suit up in the armor of God and we fight. How do we fight? Psalm 149:6 says, "God's high and holy praises fill their mouths, for their shouted praises are their weapons of war!" (TPT) Shout out praises and claim the victory.

Identity

Now for the ladies reading this, just in case you are thinking of being a warrior as a masculine trait, you'll be delighted to discover that God's design for his daughters is far better than we've ever been taught.

When God created Eve in Genesis 2, the Hebrew words to describe her are *'ezer kenegdo*. When translated to English, it was watered down to "helper" or "helpmate," but that isn't a correct description of her purpose. Women were not intended to simply be the man's helper, but this incorrect thought pattern has trapped women in secondary roles in the church and at home.

'Ezer kenegdo should actually be translated as a powerful warrior of equal worth to the man. *'Ezer* is used twenty-one times in the Bible, and it is consistently used in a military context. Sixteen of those times *'ezer* is used to describe God as Israel's helper. How cool is that?

Kenegdo means "corresponding to" or "equal to." Your strength lies in being powerfully feminine and leaning back into who Jesus created you to be. We are built with the innate ability to go to war for our loved ones, but it's time to go to war for ourselves too. Discover that there is literally nothing secondary about you. You are created in the image of God, and you are a powerful warrior full of purpose and vision.

❓ Do you walk around feeling like a warrior?

_____

_____

_____

❓ When you have an idea in your head about something you want to do in your life or would like to accomplish, do you say to yourself, *I'm a royal priest and a warrior. I have authority over this battle . . . of course I should go do that?*

_____

_____

_____

❓ Or do you think of your weaknesses instead? Why it would be hard or why it's not for you? Do you ask for a confirmation from God, and then refuse to see it when He gives it to you?

_____

_____

_____

Identity

(?) Usually the moment we decide to do something good for ourselves, every lie in our head squashes any of the feelings of goodness we may have experienced. Why is that? Why is it so hard for us to believe and act on what God says about us? I believe it is directly related to the emotional baggage we carry in our hearts.

_____

_____

_____

Designed for Joy

To give you a visual of what I'm talking about, check out the scale of emotions in the chart below, developed by Dr. David R. Hawkins.

Map of Consciousness
Developed by David R. Hawkins

The Map of Consciousness is based on a logarithmic scale that spans from 0 to 1000.

Name of Level	Energetic "Frequency"	Associated Emotional State	View of Life
Enlightenment	700-1000	Ineffable	Is
Peace	600	Bliss	Perfect
Joy	540	Serenity	Complete
Love	500	Reverence	Benign
Reason	400	Understanding	Meaningful
Acceptance	350	Forgiveness	Harmonious
Willingness	310	Optimism	Hopeful
Neutrality	250	Trust	Satisfactory
Courage	200	Affirmation	Feasible
Pride	175	Scorn	Demanding
Anger	150	Hate	Antagonistic
Desire	125	Craving	Disappointing
Fear	100	Anxiety	Frightening
Grief	75	Regret	Tragic
Apathy	50	Despair	Hopeless
Guilt	30	Blame	Evil
Shame	20	Humiliation	Miserable

Identity

In his book *Power vs. Force*, Dr. Hawkins says, "Seventy-eight percent of people live below the line of courage, and their behaviors are motivated by fear or shame, or grief or anger, etc."[vi] These low level emotions that are listed on the chart below courage make us feel heavy and hopeless.

Shame might motivate you for five minutes, but when you face a difficult challenge without tapping into faith and your true identity, motivation is hard to maintain. The low-level emotions below courage control us and keep us stuck. We may feel courageous for a hot minute but only when we align our thoughts to who God is and who He says we are that we can push through the fear to take lasting action. Without that piece of the puzzle, we always go back to thoughts like *I'm a failure!*, and the anxiety cycle continues.

❓ Think about the things you've pursued in your life that just didn't happen. List the instances you can think of when you desired change or to go for something you wanted but gave up on it? It could be a desire to lose weight or stop yelling at your kids. It could be a desire to write a song or open a restaurant. This exercise is not to make you feel bad about yourself! It's to bring awareness so you can create the change you need to move into courage and push past your perceived limitations.

Identity

Look at the Map Of Consciousness chart and pinpoint which emotion you tend to experience most often when you you face a challenge. While we may experience all of the emotions listed under courage at times, there's typically a dominant emotion that we feel most often. Mine is usually anger, but it manifests as frustration. I don't scream and yell but when I am challenged, frustration is the feeling I experience the most. I've noticed that for most people, the dominant emotion they experience is fear. The fear of upsetting others or the fear of failure will stop people in their tracks. No matter what low-level emotion you struggle with, at some point you have to rise above those feelings and move into the realm of courage in order to see yourself as God says you are.

Courage opens up a new territory of places you've never been so you can learn lessons you've never learned. It allows you to see yourself in a new way that you can't see when you stay trapped inside the bubble of unworthiness. Moving forward in courage in spite of the "giants" you face determines whether or not you enter into your personal Promised Land.

At some point Gideon had to look at the confirmations God gave him and say, *This is foreign to me. God is telling me something I don't yet see or feel yet. I have nothing but courage to offer.*

Courage is the turning point. Whether you've heard what God has said about you or not, you will come to a place in your faith, in your development, and in your identity that you will have to step into courage and face a new territory that you don't feel secure in. But you know you have to if you want to grow. If you don't, you are just adding more momentum, weight, and power to the shame, fear, anger, and grief cycle that controls you now. You can know all of this about your identity, but until you are willing to trust God's plan for you and step into courage to live in that space, your reality will stay the same. Identity lies beyond courage.

You are chosen, royalty, a priest, loved, holy, forgiven, and God's special possession. You have been called into the wonderful light to be a warrior for the kingdom of God. This is your call to courage.

Healing Work

The emotional baggage we carry leads to low level emotions that keep us stuck in old habits and patterns. It's important to become aware of the experiences in your life that contributed to where you are now.

Begin making a list of all the thoughts and memories in your life that don't match up to what God says about you. We want to uncover the areas where you have been wounded so we can reframe them and stitch them up.

It doesn't matter if it seems silly. If rude Suzy told you that you were ugly in the sixth grade, write it down. If you never felt capable of living up to your parents' expectations, write it down. If your coach told you that you weren't good enough, write it down.

In the next chapter we will learn how to give these moments to God and trade them in so He can speak truth into our situations. Let's clean out our emotional closets so we can walk with courage into our Promised Land.

CHAPTER 4
The Trade

A ll of the work you have done in the last three chapters have prepared you for this point. The tool you will learn in this chapter is profound and powerful, but you'll be amazed at how simple it is.

We are royal warriors full of purpose and worth because we are God's children and a co-heirs with Christ. That said, we often miss the truth because we are stuffed full of lies and trauma. In this chapter, we are going to learn to *release* the emotions, thoughts, and experiences that prevent us from moving toward courage.

The Trade

 Were you surprised at what came up as you did your healing work from Chapter 3?

___

___

___

 Did any old memories surface that surprised you?

___

___

___

Your Heart Brain

Did you know your heart has a brain and stores memories? Over the last few years, neuroscience has shown that, aside from your head brain called the *cephalic brain*, we also have a heart brain called the *cardiac brain* and a gut brain called the *enteric brain*. The heart brain has forty thousand neurons that can operate independently from the head brain. In 2009, Harvard Medical School explained the theory of cellular memories. The theory of cellular memories states that memories, as well as personality traits, are not only stored in the brain but also in the organs such as the heart.[vii]

The heart brain handles emotional processing, expression of values, and interpersonal connections, and identifying how you feel. So all those memories that came up as you were doing your homework are stored in your body, and your heart brain remembers them. You can think of it as a garden of memories that determines how your heart interprets information.[viii]

So let's talk about what's planted in your heart garden. Matthew 12:34 says, "For what has been stored up in your hearts will be heard in the overflow of your words" (TPT) or "out of the abundance of the heart the mouth speaks" (NIV).

You have beautiful flowers in your heart garden. I promise you that you do. You wouldn't be working through this study if you didn't. And it's important to remember those moments of pure joy, peacefulness, and love. There are memories that are planted in your heart that bring you pure joy. It may be the smell of your grandmother's apple pie or a specific moment with a loved one that brings a smile to your face. It could be moments with God where you felt His presence.

But you also have some weeds. We all do to varying degrees. It's the weeds that lead your heart astray and keep you from making powerful decisions. It's the weeds that cause you to repeat patterns that leave you feeling shame. The enemy knows your weeds and he whispers them to you. Sometimes it's to shame you, and sometimes it's to make sure you stay a victim—*Poor pitiful thing, I can't believe God let that happen to you. You deserve a treat!*—but either way he uses your weeds to make sure the filter you look through life with keeps you incapacitated and cut off from accessing the joy of your birthright.

Weeds can be cultivated in many ways. They might grow because of the expectations people have had of you. We may feel the weight of not meeting expectations of our parents, teachers, coaches, pastors, spouses, or others. It could be rejection you have felt from loved ones and friends.

Generational weeds can also grow in your garden. We can inherit the weeds of our family, either from observing their dysfunction and picking up their bad habits or by inheriting genetic physical and mental health issues that are passed through DNA. Weeds can also grow out of failed relationships like divorce, sibling rivalry, or unresolved trauma.

Weeds often grow from the expectations you have of others that didn't get met. When we need something from someone and they don't meet our expectations, it can be a painful pill to swallow. Even if our expectations of that person weren't fair or realistic, the hurt we experience can grow weeds of bitterness and resentment when our pain isn't processed properly.

Many of us don't realize that we have authority over our thoughts and our hearts, but we do. It is our responsibility to clean out the weeds and replace lies with truth. If you have a thought that doesn't inspire faith, hope, or love, it isn't from God. Weed your heart, because as you get more and more weeds, they choke out the beauty of life and cloud the filter you view life through. Eventually we put up so many walls in our heart to avoid pain and rejection that we live in just a very small room of the mansion God has available for us.

Pruning Your Heart Garden

It is incredible important to prune the garden of your heart. Romans 12:2 says, "Do not be conformed to this world, but be transformed by the renewal of your mind, that by testing you may discern what is the will of God, what is good and acceptable and perfect" (NIV). I believe that pruning your heart is a vital piece of mind renewal.

In the book *Switch On Your Brain* by Dr. Caroline Leaf, she teaches a process called the 21 Day Brain Detox. In it, you look for the lies you believe, and replace them by focusing on scripture passages that negate the lie every time your thoughts about a situation are negative. It's very similar to the exercise we did in Chapter 1 with our word picture. Neuroscience has shown that it takes twenty-one days to rewire your brain to a new thought pattern or habit, so her theory is that by day twenty-one, you will have replaced the lie with truth.

For example, I was looking at life through a filter of financial lack. Every time I had an anxious thought about money, I would say the verse Philippians 4:19, "And my God will meet all your needs according to the riches of his glory in Christ Jesus" (NIV), to work toward rewiring that thought pattern of insecurity. Her twenty-one-day plan is awesome, but by day twelve, when I wasn't seeing the change I was longing for, my consistency would slip and I would never make it the full twenty-one days. It felt like I was just laying a scripture Band-AID over a wound, because my life experience had led my heart to not really believe what I was telling it to believe. It was only when I discovered how to weed my heart and pull the roots on the lies I believed that I was able to truly see life through the proper filter of abundance.

What I discovered about myself—and have seen be true for the people I've led through this process—is that I tend to grip the situations in my life with such force that I don't release them to God. I pray about them and beg for help, and I ask for His will to be done. But the *release* of our worries to Him is what creates the change we desire. Opening our hands and our hearts releases the control, expectations, and emotions to our Heavenly Father, wholly trusting that He is working all things together for our good.

1 Peter 5:6-7, says, "Humble yourselves, therefore, under God's mighty hand, that he may lift you up in due time. Cast all your anxiety on him because he cares for you" (NIV). The word Peter uses here for "cast" is *epirrhipto,* which means "to throw upon, or place upon." Peter was a fisherman, and in order to catch fish, he had to cast his net into the water. He wouldn't have caught anything if he had kept the net in the boat and just begged for help. He had to release the net to get to the treasure.

Reciting our issues to God but refusing to release our anxieties and frustrations to Him is like keeping the net in the boat and wondering why we aren't catching any fish. We have to learn how to take our net of anxiety off our shoulders and hand it to God. Remember, you can trust God. He wants you to share your problems with Him so He can bring you restoration. He has a solution for every single worry you have, and you'll begin to see those solutions when you trust and release.

The process I use for releasing my cares to God is called "The Trade." I was introduced to this process by my friend Jennifer Hawkins. Her church has a Freedom Prayer ministry, and The Trade is a tool used to help people work through their spiritual struggles. It is a powerful way to cast your cares upon God, and I have used it over and over to pull the weeds in my heart. I believe it is effective because it involves releasing the

The Trade

situations in your life to God and asking Him to speak a fresh word into the situation.

The Trade involves analyzing your emotions about an event in your life. You will look at how the particular situation makes you feel, and then release yourself or anyone else who may have contributed to those feelings through forgiveness.

I want to stop for just a second and talk about my favorite "F" word: *forgiveness*. Forgiveness has nothing to do with approving of or justifying anyone's bad behavior. It's simply the release of the person to God. It's letting go and trusting God to deal with the situation. He knows all the working parts, and He will work every situation for your good. But in order for you to move forward in life, you have to release the person and situation to Him. Otherwise, you are just dragging the person with you everywhere you go. Last, we will surrender those feelings to God and ask Him to replace them with emotions that come from Him.

Let's get started!

The Trade

Take three deep breaths.

I want you to think about the specific situation in your life that consistently causes you the most frustration, fear, anxiety, grief, overwhelm, or other negative emotion. This might be something that you put on your healing work list from the last chapter. It could be an issue with anger, a relationship issue, a self-worth issue, or a financial issue, to name a few.

Journal in detail with complete emotional honesty what you *feel* about the situation. Write out all that you lack, why you want it to change, and your most honest thoughts about how you feel not having it.

No need to hold back. Be brutally honest. Don't filter yourself; it's okay to whine or rage. Feelings are like two-year-olds sometimes. That's ok. We can't let them drive the car but we also can't shove them in the trunk either. They have to be heard and dealt with.

Read over what you wrote, and highlight or circle the words that have the strongest emotion.

The Trade

❓ Is there another time in your life when you've felt these same emotions?

_____

_____

_____

❓ What memories from your childhood or the past does this feeling relate to?

_____

_____

_____

❓ Who needs to be forgiven in this area of your life?

_____

_____

_____

Ask God to help you forgive anyone, including yourself, who may have denied you, hurt you, overlooked you, or somehow taught you any kind of untruth, even indirectly. Remember we aren't justifying anyone's negative behavior or unjustly accusing anyone. We are just releasing the situation and the person to God so you can be set free.

"God I release _____ from the hurt they caused, the responsibility they dropped, or the untruths they taught me, and I allow you to show me or give me what is missing in my life because of that."

Surrender that feeling to God. Give that feeling to Him. Visualize yourself handing it to Him. This is you casting your cares on Him.

Tell Him that you know it's not the truth of who you are, who He is, or how He works. Tell Him that you want to see fully how He sees you and receive what's meant for you.

Now ask Him what He has to give you in return. Write down the first pictures, words, thoughts, or feelings that come to you. It doesn't have to be flashing lights, bells, whistles, or roaring thunder. It's usually subtle, so you could easily explain it away.

What word, vision, picture, or thought did you experience?

_____

_____

_____

What does it mean to you?

_____

_____

_____

The Trade

Congrats on a job well done. If you didn't get a word, don't get discouraged. Most of the time it comes immediately, but sometimes it's slower. When it's slower, it's because your analytical brain is in overdrive. It will come. Sometimes God has to talk to me in that sleepy time right before I fall asleep or right before I wake up because my brain tends to stay in overdrive.

I have used The Trade over and over again to unload burdens of untruth in my life. When I traded in my issue of financial insecurity, I explained to God that the filter of money that plagued me made me feel unstable and unsupported and not taken care of. I released my frustration to Him and asked for forgiveness for believing a lie.

Fear over finances is not something I learned from my parents, so I really didn't know who to forgive when I got to that part. I forgave myself for believing a lie, and then I forgave any of the generations before me who could have influenced the way I thought about money and stability. I had lived my whole life with more than enough, so it didn't make any sense that the story I told myself was that there was never enough and I was not going to be taken care of.

I traded all of that in, and when I asked God what I could have in return, I heard the word *bounty*. That is not a word that I ever use, so I knew it was from God. I knew that bounty was the opposite of lack, but I went on a little treasure hunt to see more about that word.

According to Merriam Webster, *bounty* is defined as "something that is given generously" or "a yield, as in the form of a crop." It is a gift or reward, especially from a higher power or government, and the word implies that the gifts are bestowed generously.

How cool is that? God reminded me that He has good gifts that He will generously bestow on me as I trust Him and release the lie that I was experiencing financial lack. That's incredible.

This didn't mean that I was going to win the lottery the next week. If I had taken the word *bounty* and set an expectation that God was going to dump a pile of money in my lap instantly, I would have missed what He was doing. Instead, the word He released set in motion the process where my brain and my heart would come into agreement with the truth of kingdom abundance. It didn't happen overnight, but now when I quote Philippians 4:19, "And my God will meet all your needs according to the riches of his glory in Christ Jesus" (NIV), I can feel the truth of the scripture all throughout my body.

Over the next few days, watch for what else He reveals to you. Let go of any expectations you may have around the word He gave you. What He has to give you is far better than what you could ask or imagine. Understand that when God speaks, He creates. So when He gives you a word, His creative power is released and it lays the foundation for you to walk toward Him in courage.

Make sure to give yourself plenty of grace, because healing is a process and it's rarely linear. If I ever have a thought that makes me feel that I'm lacking, I capture it, toss it out, and remind myself of all the scriptures that promise abundance. If you catch yourself thinking thoughts and feeling like you have in the past, remind yourself that you traded that situation or feeling in and that God has reframed it for you. Remember you are a child of the King; adjust your crown.

Also understand that when you have the courage to break these cycles, you are changing your family legacy. The cycle of dysfunction stops with you. As you trade in lies and begin to view life from the lens God designed you to see life through, your healing affects your family legacy.

Deuteronomy 7:9 says, "Know therefore that the LORD your God is God; he is the faithful God, keeping his covenant of love to a thousand generations of those who love him and keep his commandments" (NIV). God's grace is so extensive that while a few generations may experience "the sins of the father," God's covenant of mercy and grace extends to a thousand generations. Knowing that my healing unlocks healing for others is so beautiful that it inspires me to keep uncovering every thought I have that isn't in alignment with who God designed me to be.

Healing Work

One of my biggest lessons was learning to decipher what I actually have control over in my life. The main thing I learned is that the only person I have control over is *me*. God is the Father of every other person on the planet; it is not my job to control their choices. You can and should pray for the people around you, but playing God in their lives never gets you the results you want. If you want to positively impact the people around you, do the work on yourself. Your healing will radiate out of you and impact others in the most profound and beautiful ways.

As far as the situations you are trading in, it is super helpful to make a list of what you can control in the situation and what is God's to take care of. Realistically, what are the steps you can take to resolve the situation? Often, in the situations we are trading in, there's nothing we can do but release it to God and let Him restore it without us meddling and getting in the way. However, if God does reveal steps to you that you need to take, *take them*.

The Trade

❓ In the situation you traded in, what can you control? Are there any steps God is telling you to take?

_____

_____

_____

❓ In the situation you traded in, what or who is God in control of?

_____

_____

_____

Bonus Healing Work

Create a list of every person you can think of who you need to forgive for hurting you or making you feel unworthy throughout your life. Start in your childhood and work your way up through the years. You should be able to pull some names from the last chapter's healing work.

When you get your list written out, forgive and release those people. Imagine yourself literally cutting the cords that attach them to you. You aren't cutting those people out of your life, but you are creating a visual moment where you are detaching from the weight of those comments, situations, and people who hurt you.

When you are finished, tear up the list and throw it away, or burn it if you're feeling especially sassy. I promise you that this exercise will make you feel so much lighter in your spirit.

CHAPTER 5
Supernatural Sight

I don't know about you, but I'm a get-to-the-destination-as fast-as-possible kind of girl. But I've discovered that most of life is about the process of getting there. No matter how fast I want life to go, things don't always move on my timetable. Same goes with growth and healing.

The word or picture or vision you get from God is where He's taking you, but it's a process to get to the palace and healing is rarely linear. We tend to want constant forward progress, and we get super discouraged and defeated if we slide backward. When we realize that healing is a process and we need to have grace for ourselves, we can relax on the journey. You wouldn't get mad at a baby for falling as they are learning how to walk. Healing involves patience, trust, and continually pulling His word for your life into your reality…on earth as it is in heaven.

This chapter is about living from a supernatural perspective because you are in a war for your word. When God gives you a fresh perspective that doesn't match up with what you currently see in front of you, you need tools to help you see with supernatural eyesight. Cleaning out your emotional baggage does wonders for living a lighter, more joyful lifestyle, but we also need practical tools to build our faith muscles while we are waiting for the restoration we long for.

The War You Are In

You are warring against yourself. Your subconscious mind is so programmed to behave certain ways and think specific thoughts that you have to continually remind yourself of who God is and who He says you are until it becomes automatic. Remember, it takes twenty-one days to create new thought pathways. Write the word or picture that God gave you and the scriptures that support it down and post it in your house, your car, and on your phone. Wherever you can see it constantly and be reminded to hold onto hope.

We are in a war against culture. We get so much negative noise from the media pushing fear and disaster. We have so much noise from advertising, TV, and movies telling us how we should look to be beautiful and accepted. Everyone has an agenda, and they are pushing their message at us over and over again. If the message you are getting from the news is causing you to fall into fear, stop watching it. If the message from a TV show is telling you that you aren't skinny enough, pretty enough, or wholly accepted in the eyes of God, stop watching it. Learn to set healthy boundaries on the things that rob you of your peace. I stopped watching the news years ago and it is glorious. I can't stand to hear the fear spewing through the screen and trying to take away my power. I refuse to buy what they are selling, and my life is much more peaceful because of it.

You are also in a war for your word against the enemy. The enemy knows when your spirit surges with hope, and the pleasure of his existence is to bring you down. You may notice that your situation gets worse before it gets better once you release it and get your word. Spiritual warfare is a real thing, but remember: you have all authority over Satan. He can huff and puff, but if you wield your authority as a Royal Warrior, he can't blow your house down.

God Works in Mysterious Ways

It's important to understand that God works in mysterious ways. There are times that He will tell you to do something about your situation that you don't quite understand. Even if it seems counterintuitive and strange, obedience to Him brings you the exact breakthrough you desire. I'm going to give you two biblical examples of what I'm talking about.

Remember when God spoke to Gideon and told him that he was a warrior and God would use him to do the thing for Israel that would bring peace to the people? Judges 6:16 says, "The Lord answered, 'I will be with you, and you will strike down all the Midianites, leaving none alive'" (NIV). One would think that would mean that Gideon would take a massive army into the Midianite camp and defeat them with weapons, but that's not how it went down. Let's look at how God told him to do this:

> Early in the morning, Jerub-Baal (that is, Gideon) and all his men camped at the spring of Harod. The camp of Midian was north of them in the valley near the hill of Moreh. The LORD said to Gideon, "You have too many men. I cannot deliver Midian into their hands, or Israel would boast against me, 'My own strength has saved me.' Now announce to the army, 'Anyone who trembles with fear may turn back and leave Mount Gilead.'" So twenty-two thousand men left, while ten thousand remained.
>
> But the LORD said to Gideon, "There are still too many men. Take them down to the water, and I will thin them out for you there. If I say, 'This one shall go with you,' he shall go; but if I say, 'This one shall not go with you,' he shall not go."

So Gideon took the men down to the water. There the LORD told him, "Separate those who lap the water with their tongues as a dog laps from those who kneel down to drink." Three hundred of them drank from cupped hands, lapping like dogs. All the rest got down on their knees to drink.

The LORD said to Gideon, "With the three hundred men that lapped I will save you and give the Midianites into your hands. Let all the others go home." So Gideon sent the rest of the Israelites home but kept the three hundred, who took over the provisions and trumpets of the others.

Now the camp of Midian lay below him in the valley. During that night the LORD said to Gideon, "Get up, go down against the camp, because I am going to give it into your hands. If you are afraid to attack, go down to the camp with your servant Purah and listen to what they are saying. Afterward, you will be encouraged to attack the camp." So he and Purah his servant went down to the outposts of the camp. The Midianites, the Amalekites and all the other eastern peoples had settled in the valley, thick as locusts. Their camels could no more be counted than the sand on the seashore.

Gideon arrived just as a man was telling a friend his dream. "I had a dream," he was saying. "A round loaf of barley bread came tumbling into the Midianite camp. It struck the tent with such force that the tent overturned and collapsed."

His friend responded, "This can be nothing other than the sword of Gideon son of Joash, the Israelite. God has given the Midianites and the whole camp into his hands."

When Gideon heard the dream and its interpretation, he bowed down and worshiped. He returned to the camp of Israel and called out, "Get up! The LORD has given the Midianite camp into your hands." Dividing the three hundred men into three companies, he placed trumpets and empty jars in the hands of all of them, with torches inside.

"Watch me," he told them. "Follow my lead. When I get to the edge of the camp, do exactly as I do. When I and all who are with me blow our trumpets, then from all around the camp blow yours and shout, 'For the LORD and for Gideon.'"

Gideon and the hundred men with him reached the edge of the camp at the beginning of the middle watch, just after they had changed the guard. They blew their trumpets and broke the jars that were in their hands. The three companies blew the trumpets and smashed the jars. Grasping the torches in their left hands and holding in their right hands the trumpets they were to blow, they shouted, "A sword for the LORD and for Gideon!" While each man held his position around the camp, all the Midianites ran, crying out as they fled.

When the three hundred trumpets sounded, the LORD caused the men throughout the camp to turn on each other with their swords. The army fled to Beth Shittah toward Zererah as far as the border of Abel Meholah near Tabbath. Israelites from Naphtali, Asher and all Manasseh were called out, and they pursued the Midianites. Gideon sent messengers throughout the hill country of Ephraim, saying, "Come down against the Midianites and seize the waters of the Jordan ahead of them as far as Beth Barah."

So all the men of Ephraim were called out and they seized the waters of the Jordan as far as Beth Barah. They also captured two of the Midianite leaders, Oreb and Zeeb. They killed Oreb at the rock of Oreb, and Zeeb at the winepress of Zeeb. They pursued the Midianites and brought the heads of Oreb and Zeeb to Gideon, who was by the Jordan. (Judges 7, NIV)

Okay, I hope you read this whole passage and didn't just glance over it, because there's some excellent stuff here. God reduced Gideon's army from thirty-two thousand men to three-hundred men. He knew Gideon was afraid, so He gave him a way to receive encouragement and confirmation. Gideon's army of three hundred men used trumpets, empty jars, and torches as weapons. And they won the battle. They didn't even have to fight! God did everything because they followed His strange commands.

God does not fight battles the way we do. We are limited in what we can see, but God sees outside of space and time. His solutions are going to be different. We just have to trust Him when they don't make sense to us.

Here's another example. Remember when Joshua was leading the Isrealites into the Promised Land, and the first giant they had to overcome was Jericho? Look at how God told them to take down the walls of Jericho:

> Now the gates of Jericho were securely barred because of the Israelites. No one went out and no one came in.
>
> Then the LORD said to Joshua, "See, I have delivered Jericho into your hands, along with its king and its fighting men. March around the city once with all the armed men. Do this for six days. Have seven priests carry trumpets of rams' horns in front of the ark. On the seventh day, march around the city seven times, with the priests blowing the trumpets. When you hear them sound a long blast on the trumpets, have the whole army give a loud shout; then the wall of the city will collapse and the army will go up, everyone straight in. (Joshua 6:1-5, NIV)

Joshua followed God's bizarre instructions for battle, and "when the trumpets sounded, the army shouted, and at the sound of the trumpet, when the men gave a loud shout, the wall collapsed; so everyone charged straight in, and they took the city" (v. 20).

Once again, there were strange instructions, odd weapons, and zero fighting . . . but total breakthrough occurred. When we trust God, listen to what He says, and *do* what He says, we don't even have to fight the battle. The walls of our issue collapse under His direction.

In March 2019, fairly soon after I received the word *bounty* from God, I was praying one day about my job at the salon. I heard God clearly say that I was to leave my job by May 31. This was something I had wanted to do for a long time, but my filter of financial lack couldn't even see it as a true possibility. My thoughts would immediately go to how irresponsible that would be. My analytical brain would rabbit trail, and I would wonder how in the world we pay our bills. Next thing you know, I would be thinking through how we would have to sell our house and we would be homeless. OK, maybe it wasn't that drastic, but seriously, I was nervous.

On top of that, I had to tell my friends and family that I was leaving my job, and I knew they would think I was insane. Who quits a job that you've done for seventeen years and pays well? God knows me, and He knew I would need serious confirmation to make this step. I had been praying about this for a long time, but I couldn't see how it was possible. Even though moving on was something I desperately wanted, all I could think of were all the reasons it wouldn't work.

Right after I finished praying, my phone dinged with a YouTube notification. A woman whose videos I follow was telling all about how she started her ministry and a couple years later God told her husband to leave his high-powered corporate job to help her in her ministry. He was nervous because he wasn't sure how they would pay their bills and both of their cars would be taken away because they were company cars. She told him that if God called him to it they would be insane not to listen; all those details would get worked out. Her message was all about how God had taken care of them and had given them more than they could have imagined. That was my first major confirmation.

Then I began getting crazy rashes from hair color. I would go to work and my face would swell up and turn red after I worked on a few clients. I had never had allergies before, so it was just so strange. It was like God was cornering me from all sides and giving me every reason to be obedient to what He was calling me to do.

So I did it. I was courageous and I quit my job. It was terrifying and exhilarating all at the same time. But it wasn't until I was obedient with quitting my job that I got my next assignment, which was writing this study on everything I had learned about my identity in Christ so others could choose to live as powerful warriors too.

Now as God unveils the next step to you, it will require courage. There's so much noise we have to silence as we walk toward our breakthroughs. The process of writing this hasn't been all roses and sunshine. I've been frustrated, confused, and wondered who in the world would listen to anything I have to say. I've used excuses like, *I don't have time to write* and *Who am I to write this book?* even though I know it was my assignment to do it. All of these feelings could have kept me frozen, so I set a plan in place to propel me forward when the negative thoughts would ramp up.

I'm going to list out the methods I continually use to pull myself up when I start slipping into noise and negativity. It's important for you to have your own plan for maintaining your supernatural eyesight. I've got lots of options for you to choose from, so pick the ones that resonate with you and strengthen you. Let's go ahead and make your plan now so you'll be able to stand strong.

Time with God

Spend time daily with God. Not as a to-do to mark off your list, but because it is the only way to get real fulfillment. Something beautiful happens when we lean back and let Him pour life into us daily. When you soak in His presence on a regular basis, you will begin to recognize the feeling of true alignment and you will crave time with Him in order to find your equilibrium. I'm still learning to follow the prompts the Holy Spirit nudges at my heart. Some days I'm better at it than others. When I get frustrated about that, I remind myself that growth is rarely linear and I have a little compassion for myself.

Is there a specific time of day that you can get to yourself and spend some time with God?

_____

_____

_____

My preference is first thing in the morning before the kids get up, but if my day doesn't allow for that, I will take a walk or a bath and spend some time talking with God about what's going on in my life and how I feel about it.

Find a Confidant

Find a friend or family member to walk through this process with you. Tell them your struggles and be vulnerable. Everyone has crap they are struggling with. We live in a broken world and it comes with the territory, but everything seems scarier in the dark. When we unload our burdens and bring them into the light, we can be there for each other.

Pick someone who will remind you that you are a warrior and you do the same for them. Hold each other's arms up when you get tired like Aaron and Hur did for Moses (Exodus 17). My friend Jennifer and I have spent countless hours on the Voxer app talking back and forth and holding each other's arms up. I truly can't imagine walking through life without someone who you can share your thoughts with. We all need someone to remind us when we are off track and celebrate with us when we experience a breakthrough.

Who will you partner with in this process?

_____

_____

_____

If you can't currently think of someone in your life to walk with, ask God to bring you that person. He will do it!

What You Can Control

We talked about this in the Healing Work section in the last chapter, but this is so important I want to repeat it again. We tend to be control freaks, and this is such a helpful tool. In every circumstance, make a list of what is yours to control and what you need to release to God. Only focus on what is on your list! Leave the rest up to Him. It is not your job to change the situation or anyone else. They belong to God, and He is fighting those battles for you. Your only job is to follow Him and do what He tells you to do.

Make this list and keep it right in front of you as a reminder to *let it go* if it's not yours to carry. If it's not good yet, it's not the end.

List of Testimonies

Make a list of personal testimonies of when God has been there for you and read them every time you get fearful. What has God done for you in the past? This is so powerful! If He did it before, He will do it again. Maybe not in the same way, but the reminder of His faithfulness to you will pull you through when you are feeling fearful or discouraged.

I also find it helpful to make a list of other people's testimonies. If you desire to see your marriage restored, make a list of other people whose marriages God has restored. If you desire to find your purpose in life, make a list of all the people you know who are walking in their purpose. The Word says God is no respecter of persons, which means if he did it for someone else He will do it for you.

Tune your antenna to where God has worked or is working. We find what we are looking for. Look for the miracles and you'll find more of them. The miracles will keep you from sinking.

Meditate

As Joshua is getting ready to enter the Promised Land, God tells him that the recipe for being prosperous and successful is to meditate on the Word day and night. Joshua 1:8 says, "Keep this Book of the Law always on your lips; meditate on it day and night, so that you may be careful to do everything written in it. Then you will be prosperous and successful" (NIV).

One of my favorite tools for Christian meditation is the Soultime Meditation app. This app was developed by Danny Silk and it is phenomenal. You'll find meditations based on God's Word that help you with a variety of topics such as: sleep, anxiety, finding your purpose, and so on. Download the app and use it daily.

Do you meditate on the Word daily?

_____

_____

_____

Fill Your Head and Heart with Hope

I am obsessed with filling my head and heart full of hope, and I know that I am personally responsible for the messages I take in. Instead of the news, I listen to podcasts that fill me full of faith and remind me of the God I serve. My favorite podcasts for this are the Bethel Church sermon of the week and Kris Vallotton's podcast. Find what fills you up and think on those things. You can also check out my podcast, "Metamorphosis." The purpose of the podcast is to help people unload their emotional baggage and walk forward in faith. You get to choose what you focus on. Choose faith over fear.

What podcasts, speakers, worship music, or pastors are you going to listen to when you need a boost?

_____

_____

_____

Speak Life

Watch the words you speak. You were created in the image of the Master Creator. And how does He create? With His words. He speaks and life happens. What we don't realize is that we do the same. The words we speak over ourselves, our situations, the people in our lives, and our progress *matter*. Everything we say carries creative power because we are made in His image. Proverbs 18:21 says, "Death and life are in the power of the tongue: and they that love it shall eat the fruit thereof" (KJV).

How does God describe Himself when Moses asks Him who He is? I AM. And how do you describe yourself? I am sick, I am ugly, I am not good enough, I can't do it, I am stuck, and so on. You are literally speaking death over yourself. Or how about your spouse? He is so difficult or lazy. I wish he was a better provider, father, healthier. Or how about our situations? It is impossible, it is terminal, it is hopeless?

It's time to start speaking life over every aspect of your existence. Begin to decree and declare truth over yourself. Take responsibility for the words you speak, and *speak life*.

What do you speak over yourself that needs to stop?

_____

_____

_____

Repeat after me . . . "I am loved. I am chosen. I am favored. I matter. By His stripes I am healed. I am a warrior. I am thriving. I am prosperous. I am protected. I am the head and not the tail. I am blessed. I have purpose. I am a warrior. I can do all things through Christ who strengthens me. I have purpose. I am creative. I am full of wisdom. God is good and He is in control.

Speak these words over yourself, your spouse, your kids, and your situations *every single day.*

Gratitude

We tend to find what we are looking for. Begin each day looking for the good. I like to make a list of at least five things I'm thankful for every morning. It doesn't have to be profound. In fact, coffee makes my list most days. Just think on the good and watch it multiply.

List at least five things you are grateful for today.

_____

_____

_____

Expect Warfare

Expect spiritual warfare. When you start waking up and you realize that the "reality" you see is an illusion and you actually have authority over the enemy, you are his nightmare. This could sound scary, but you have authority.

Luke 10:19 says, "Behold, I have given you authority to tread on serpents and scorpions, and over all the power of the enemy, and nothing shall hurt you" (ESV). God has not given us a spirit of fear. Fear is a spirit, so cast that spirit out with your words in the name of Jesus. Cast it out and decree and declare God's promises over yourself.

❓ Are there specific areas in your life where you are experiencing warfare? Any thoughts you are having that don't inspire faith, hope, and love?

_____

_____

_____

When you recognize the warfare affecting you, tell the enemy to go away and begin to speak truth over yourself.

Growth is a Continual Journey

This is a never-ending process. Holding tight to joy and freedom isn't always easy, but it's much easier than the alternative of living in fear. As you walk this process out, you will begin to notice the minute you get out of alignment and you will crave finding that spot again. When that happens, go back and use the tools above and find your sweet spot. When the hope floods back in, you'll know you are there.

Designed for Joy

Ephesians 3:16-17 says, "And I pray that he would unveil within you the unlimited riches of his glory and favor until supernatural strength floods your innermost being with his divine might and explosive power. Then, by constantly using your faith, the life of Christ will be released deep inside you, and the resting place of his love will become the very source and root of your life" (TPT).

You were designed for *joy*. I pray that you feel it and it radiates out of you.

Thank you for walking toward healing with me. I can't wait to see the beautiful growth that happens within you.

Resources

Tools for Freedom: 21-Day Prayer Journal

My favorite tool for creating awareness and moving stagnant emotions out is with certified pure therapeutic grade essential oils. We know that it takes twenty-one days to create a new thought pattern or instill a new healthy habit. Jennifer and I created this journal to help you walk through The Trade and process the emotions that come up. Using essential oils makes the shift easier and more profound. You can find the journal at www.valpetty.com or our podcast website, www.valandjen.com.

If you don't have certified pure therapeutic grade essential oils, you can still use the journal. Just follow the prompts and you'll be good to go. If you want to learn more about using essential oils to process emotions, follow my

Facebook group and Instagram page, The Essential Joyologist, and subscribe to our podcast, "Metamorphosis."

You can reach out to me at www.valpetty.com for personal guidance using essential oils.

Connect with Me

Website: www.valpetty.com

Facebook: The Essential Joyologist:
https://www.facebook.com/groups/630793240325313/?ref=bookmarks

Instagram: Val Petty—The Essential Joyologist:
https://www.instagram.com/valpetty/

Endnotes

[i] Dr. Caroline Leaf, *Switch On Your Brain* (Ada, MI: Baker Books) 33-34.

[ii] https://www.goodreads.com/quotes/376518-what-comes-into-our-minds-when-we-think-about-god

[iii] Dan Harris and Enjoli Francis, "A Look at the 4 Ways Americans View God," *ABCNews.com*, October 7, 2010, https://abcnews.go.com/WN/book-religion-examines-ways-americans-perceive-god/story?id=11825319

[iv] Alyssa Roat, "What Does Agape Love Really Mean in the Bible?" *Christianity Today*, https://www.christianity.com/wiki/christian-terms/what-does-agape-love-really-mean-in-the-bible.html

[v] Shari Abbott, "The Names of Jehovah Hidden in Psalm 21!", Reasons for Hope, https://reasonsforhopejesus.com/names-jehovah-hidden-psalm-23/

[vi] David R. Hawkins, *Power vs. Force* (Carlsbad, CA: Hay House, 2014) 90-91.

[vii] Gianna Absi, "Is the brain the only place that stores our memories?" *The Nerve Blog*, https://sites.bu.edu/ombs/2014/11/11/is-the-brain-the-only-place-that-stores-our-memories/

[viii] "Head, Heart, and Guts: The Three Brains that Control Our Intuition," *InvisibleEdge.com*, https://invisible-edgellc.com/head-heart-gut/

Made in the USA
Coppell, TX
03 July 2020